AF679477

The 3 Dimensions of Wealth Workbook

By Dennis Doboyouh

Table of Contents

By Dennis Doboyouh

This is My Story

My name is Dennis Doboyouh, and my journey begins in the place I once called home: Liberia, a nation on the West African coast, known for its deep green forests, vibrant cultures, and an enduring spirit passed down through generations. I was born into a country full of promise, one shaped by a rich tapestry of traditions, extended family bonds, and communal living. Yet, my homeland's beauty stood in stark contrast to the storm brewing in the late 1980s. I grew up during a tumultuous era, one in which political instability and social unrest bubbled ominously beneath the surface of everyday life. In 1990, these tensions reached a breaking point, and Liberia was engulfed in a brutal civil war that would eventually force me and millions of others to abandon everything we knew.

Before the war, life in Liberia was not without its challenges, but there was a sense of normalcy and hope. As a child, my world revolved around my immediate family, my neighbors, and the everyday routines that gave structure to my life. Morning chores, attending school, spending afternoons playing soccer or simply sitting under mango trees sharing stories—all these small moments formed the backdrop of my youth. Liberia's cultural rhythms were diverse and layered, a tapestry of languages, customs, and religious faiths. I remember the laughter of relatives gathering for family occasions, the aroma of jollof rice wafting from the kitchen, and the pride I felt in being part of a community where everyone looked out for each other.

The outbreak of civil war in 1990 tore that peaceful existence asunder. Armed conflict is not merely a matter of political headlines; it reaches into people's homes and hearts, carving deep scars that often take a lifetime to heal. The war in Liberia was ferocious and merciless. It claimed the lives of hundreds of thousands and forced even more to flee. As the violence closed in, the question wasn't whether to leave but how. Staying meant risking your life daily. The day came when I knew I had to go, and with tears in my eyes and uncertainty gnawing at my soul, I joined the mass exodus of people searching for refuge and a glimmer of hope beyond Liberia's borders.

For me, and for countless others, that refuge lay in Côte d'Ivoire, just to the east. Crossing the border was a surreal journey—on the one hand, it represented salvation from the violence, yet on the other, it meant leaving home and venturing into the unknown. The refugee experience is difficult to describe. Imagine being uprooted from everything familiar and placed in a camp with thousands of people who share your plight. Some are neighbors, other strangers, but all are bound together by trauma and loss. The refugee camps in Côte d'Ivoire offered a semblance of safety, but life there was far from easy. There were long lines for food and water, basic medical care was scarce, and finding any sense of normalcy required resilience and resourcefulness.

I spent a decade in Côte d'Ivoire as a refugee—ten long years that would shape my character, test my faith, and eventually illuminate a path forward. In the early days, I struggled with fear, uncertainty, and a lingering sense of displacement. However, I refused to let these feelings define me. Instead, I turned inward, drawing on the faith and values my family had instilled in me. I had always believed in the power of education, seeing it not only to personal advancement but as a vehicle for understanding the world and one's place in it. Even in the camp, I focused on academic self-improvement. Whenever I could, I found ways to study, to read, and to learn new skills. Education, even in such a haphazard environment, became a lifeline—something stable and productive I could hold on to amidst chaos.

My Christian faith played a crucial role during these years as well. I started attending small gatherings of believers in the camp. Under makeshift tents and in rudimentary chapels, we prayed together, read the Bible, and encouraged one another. There was a special kind of solidarity within the church community in the refugee camp: a shared understanding that no matter how broken our world seemed, God still cared, and He still guided the willing heart. Over time, my involvement in the church deepened. I took on roles in ministry, helping to organize worship, lead prayers, and offer counsel to those struggling even more than I was. The church was a beacon of light, and in serving it, I discovered leadership qualities within myself I did not know existed.

It was during this period that I embarked on one of my life's most meaningful projects. Witnessing children—innocent victims of the conflict—grow up with barely the basics moved me to action. Many of these children had lost parents or had been separated from them; others had never set foot in a classroom. They lacked food, clothing, shelter, and, perhaps most tragically, any real sense of a future. I decided that I could not simply stand by and watch. Drawing on the meager resources available and seeking support from fellow refugees and any kind-hearted individuals I could find, I started a humanitarian organization called Life 4 Kids.

Life 4 Kids began modestly, with a few volunteers and small contributions. Our priority was meeting basic needs: providing food, clothing, and a safe place to sleep. As we became more established, we added educational support, makeshift classrooms, and play areas. We also offered spiritual guidance, making sure that these children knew they were loved and valued, despite their harsh circumstances. There were countless challenges—funding was always scarce, resources often insufficient—but every time I saw a child smile because they had a meal or learned how to write their name, I felt a surge of purpose. Over the years, Life 4 Kids would reach hundreds of refugee children, helping to restore some of the childhood stolen by war and displacement.

Looking back, those ten years as a refugee in Côte d'Ivoire were a crucible of transformation for me. I had left Liberia with nothing, yet I gained an education of the mind and heart. I learned that adversity could refine instead of breaking a person, that faith could serve as an anchor in the storm, and that service to others could bring meaning to suffering. I learned how to lead, to build, to organize, and most importantly, to see hope where others only saw despair. These lessons would serve me well when the next great opportunity in my life arrived.

In 1999, after nearly a decade in exile, fortune smiled upon me in the form of the U.S. Diversity Visa Lottery—often known simply as the DV Lottery. Winning this lottery was more than just a stroke of luck. It represented a chance to rebuild my life in a place that promised greater stability, opportunity, and freedom. My heart was filled with gratitude and anticipation. With the DV paperwork in order, I prepared to migrate to the United States in August 1999. I traveled with my family, knowing that a new chapter lay ahead.

Arriving in the United States was both thrilling and daunting. My mind buzzed with questions: How would we adapt? Would I find work? Would I be able to continue my education, my ministry, and my community work in this new land? Adjusting to American life took time. There were cultural differences to navigate, a new climate to get used to, and a whole new system to understand—from how to find housing and open a bank account to how to enroll children in school. Thankfully, I was not alone. America is a nation of immigrants, and I quickly discovered support networks, church communities, and immigrant resource centers that helped ease the transition.

One of my earliest professional opportunities came in 2000, when I was given a chance to enter the financial industry by a remarkable institution: Citizens Trust Bank. This bank, a minority-owned institution in Atlanta, Georgia, opened the door that would lead to a long and successful career in banking and finance. I started by learning the fundamentals of the banking industry—customer service, basic lending principles, financial regulations, and the importance of community engagement.

Stepping into the financial world marked a significant turning point. Over time, I moved from one position to another, each role presenting new challenges and opportunities to grow. My early experiences in mortgage lending were especially formative. I started as a mortgage loan officer, where I learned the intricacies of home loans, underwriting standards, and the responsibilities that come with helping families finance their dream homes. After a few years, I transitioned from mortgage to retail banking, a move that broadened my skill set. Handling everyday transactions, assisting customers with their financial plans, advising on saving and investment options, and guiding them toward financial stability became my daily routine. I discovered great satisfaction in helping people understand their finances and achieve their goals—whether it was opening a first savings account, navigating a new credit line, or securing a loan for a small business start-up.

Throughout my career, I had the privilege of working with some of the top financial institutions in the United States. I gained experience at JP Morgan Chase Mortgage Corporation, National City Mortgage Corporation, Wells Fargo Bank, and ultimately Bank of America, where I now serve as a Senior Banker. Each of these institutions enriched my perspective, teaching me different aspects of the industry, exposing me to varying corporate cultures, and challenging me to continually refine my financial acumen.

But my professional life in banking was never just about climbing the corporate ladder. My upbringing and my experiences as a refugee and humanitarian have always reminded me that wealth and stability mean little if not shared for the greater good. Even as I worked in these prestigious institutions, I remained deeply involved in church and community service. My spiritual life, nurtured back in the refugee camp and strengthened through years of faith in action, compelled me to be more than just a banker. Eventually, this spiritual calling led me to pastoral service.

I became a pastor at New Hope Independent Methodist Church in Atlanta, Georgia. Leading a congregation in a major American city was both a privilege and a responsibility I embraced wholeheartedly. Being a pastor allowed me to bring together my various passions—my faith, my desire to serve, and my understanding of community needs. In Atlanta, a city rich with cultural diversity, I encountered individuals from all walks of life. Many parishioners had their own stories of struggle, loss, and hope. Some were immigrants like me, searching for spiritual guidance in an unfamiliar land. Others were lifelong residents, facing different challenges—financial hardship, family issues, or personal crises. My role as a pastor was to listen, to pray with them, to advise them, and to empower them to find their own paths to healing and growth.

Serving as a pastor in Atlanta also reminded me that spiritual health, financial stability, and personal development are deeply interconnected. I saw how spiritual teachings could provide a moral compass and sense of purpose. I learned how financial education could enable families to break cycles of poverty and instability. And I realized how personal growth—academic, professional, and emotional—could lift individuals out of difficult circumstances. These three dimensions of wealth, as I would come to call them—spiritual, financial, and personal—formed the foundation of my philosophy and my life's work.

To better serve my congregation, clients, and community in an age where information and commerce increasingly live in the digital realm, I decided to further my education in a new field: cybersecurity. Completing cybersecurity training was not just a professional move—it was a practical response to the world's evolving challenges. With so many aspects of our lives now online, protecting personal information and sensitive data is paramount. This knowledge allows me to offer better guidance to the individuals and organizations I serve. Whether it's teaching a small church group how to recognize phishing scams or advising local nonprofit organizations on best practices for data protection, my cybersecurity skills ensure that I remain relevant and helpful in the modern world.

My life has not been without personal struggles. I have faced disappointments, setbacks, and heartbreak. Among these was the painful experience of going through a divorce. The end of a marriage is never easy. It brings with it feelings of loss, failure, and sadness. Yet, just as my time in the refugee camps taught me resilience, so too did this personal challenge. I learned that endings, while painful, can also open the door to new beginnings. Through prayer, reflection, and the support of friends, family, and my church community, I found healing. Today, I remain hopeful about the future and the possibility of finding love and partnership again.

I am blessed with four beautiful daughters, each of whom is carving out her own path in life. Watching them grow, guiding them through their own journeys, and helping them understand the value of faith, hard work, and compassion is one of my greatest joys. In addition to my biological children, I have countless "spiritual children"—young people in my church, my community, and beyond—whom I have mentored, counseled, or assisted over the years. I see in them the future, the possibility of a better world, and it warms my heart to know that I can play even a small part in helping them realize their potential.

Reflecting on my journey—from a boy growing up in Liberia, to a refugee in Côte d'Ivoire, to an immigrant building a new life in America—I am struck by the recurring themes of faith, perseverance, and service. Each stage of my life has taught me something essential about what it means to be human. In Liberia, I learned the importance of community and cultural identity. In Côte d'Ivoire, I learned how to adapt, to serve others in adversity, and to never give up hope. In the United States, I learned about opportunity, diversity, and the power of education and professional growth.

My calling now is to share these lessons. I am passionate about educating people on the importance of a fulfilled spiritual life—knowing that purpose and meaning transcend material possessions. I am equally passionate about teaching financial stability—helping people understand money, credit, savings, and investment, so they can build a secure foundation for themselves and their families. Finally, I emphasize continuous growth in every area of life—spiritual, intellectual, professional, and emotional—because learning and evolving are what keep us alive and engaged with the world around us.

For those who find themselves facing obstacles, I offer my story as a testament that no matter how difficult your starting point is, progress is possible. To refugees who may be reading these words, I say: Your current circumstances do not define you. Education, faith, service, and resilience can lead you beyond your present struggles. To immigrants who are trying to find their place in a new country, I encourage patience, openness to learning, and a willingness to embrace new opportunities. To those seeking financial security, I offer my experience as an example: Start small, educate yourself, build trust, and serve your community—this is how you can create a legacy of prosperity. To those who have experienced heartbreak and loss, I remind you that pain can lead to growth, and that hope, and love can be rediscovered.

Over the years, I have come to understand that life's trials and triumphs are rarely separate chapters. They are woven together, each thread adding to the tapestry of who we are. My tapestry includes the threads of war and displacement, of faith and leadership, of education and service, of professional accomplishment and personal heartache. It includes the bright colors of community, the deep hues of endurance, and the shimmering accents of hard-earned success. I have tried to weave these threads together into something meaningful, something I can share with others to inspire and uplift them.

Today, as a Senior Banker at Bank of America, I use my skills and experiences to help individuals and families manage their finances and plan for their futures. As a pastor at New Hope Independent Methodist Church, I guide people toward spiritual growth and moral integrity. As a mentor, I encourage young people to discover their strengths, set goals, and believe in their dreams. As a former refugee, I advocate for compassion, understanding, and support for those displaced by conflict and hardship. As a father, I set an example for my daughters and my spiritual children, showing them that perseverance, honesty, and empathy can illuminate even the darkest path.

I remain connected to my roots—my homeland of Liberia and the lessons learned in the refugee camps of Côte d'Ivoire. Although I live and work in the United States, I carry Liberia within me. I remember the smells, the songs, the stories, and the laughter that existed before the war. I remember the faces of friends lost and the resilience of those who survived. My heritage and my history guide my moral compass. They inspire me to approach everyone I meet—whether in a bank lobby, a church pew, or a community event—with respect, kindness, and a willingness to help.

In time, I hope to write more about my experiences, perhaps author books or create educational programs that blend spiritual wisdom with financial literacy and personal development strategies. I believe that helping others align their spiritual life with their financial and personal growth can transform individuals, families, and even communities. When people have a spiritual foundation, they treat themselves and others with dignity and compassion. When they have financial stability, they make better decisions and can invest in their families, their education, and their future. When they commit to continuous growth, they become problem-solvers, innovators, and leaders who contribute positively to society.

If I can play even a small part in guiding people toward these three dimensions of wealth—spiritual fulfillment, financial stability, and holistic growth—then I know my life has served a purpose greater than myself. I give thanks to God for every opportunity, every challenge, and every blessing He has placed on my path. I thank my family, my mentors, my congregation, and my community for their support and for inspiring me to keep striving, learning, and serving.

As I look toward the future, I see an ever-changing world. Globalization, technology, and shifting economic landscapes will continue to shape how we live, work, and connect with one another. Spiritual needs will remain constant, even if the ways we worship and gather evolve. Financial systems will adapt to new regulations, technologies, and customer expectations. People will continue to migrate, seeking safety and opportunity, just as I once did. My role is to navigate these changes with grace and courage, remaining true to the values that have guided me thus far.

I am hopeful. Hopeful about getting married again, building a loving partnership rooted in faith and shared purpose. Hopeful about my daughters' futures, knowing that they will bring their own gifts to the world. Hopeful about my community, confident that as we learn and grow together, we can tackle challenges and uplift one another. Hopeful about the larger human family, believing that empathy, understanding, and cooperation can heal wounds and bridge divides.

Introduction to The 3 Dimensions of Wealth Workbook

1 Corinthians 13:11

When I was a child, I used to speak like a child, think like a child, reason like a child; when I became a man, I did away with childish things.

Maternal Wealth, Spiritual Wealth, and Financial Wealth

Wealth, in its truest sense, is far more than material possessions or the balance in a bank account. It transcends money to encompass aspects of life that deeply enrich our existence: the nurturing influence of maternal wealth, the profound fulfillment of spiritual wealth, and the empowering freedom of financial wealth. When these three dimensions are understood, balanced, and cultivated, they form the foundation for a life of holistic abundance.

The 3 Dimensions of Wealth Workbook invites you on a journey to explore these interconnected realms of wealth. This is not a guide to achieving mere material success; it is a comprehensive tool for creating a balanced, meaningful, and fulfilling life. Each dimension—maternal, spiritual, and financial wealth—holds unique value and, when nurtured together, leads to a richer and more harmonious existence.

This introduction will lay the groundwork for understanding these dimensions, their significance, and how this workbook can serve as a guide to unlocking their full potential.

Why Explore the 3 Dimensions of Wealth?

Modern life often compels us to prioritize one aspect of wealth—usually financial—at the expense of others. While financial stability is essential, the pursuit of material gains without emotional and spiritual grounding often leaves individuals feeling empty and disconnected. Conversely, focusing solely on relationships or spirituality without financial planning can lead to instability and stress.

By integrating maternal, spiritual, and financial wealth, we create a life of balance and purpose. Each dimension complements the others, offering a framework for achieving lasting prosperity and fulfillment. This workbook provides the tools, exercises, and insights to help you align these dimensions, ensuring that your life reflects your highest values and aspirations.

The 3 Dimensions of Wealth

Maternal Wealth: The Nurturing Dimension

Maternal wealth represents the emotional and relational wealth derived from nurturing connections and relationships. While the term "maternal" traditionally refers to motherhood, in this context, it expands to include all forms of nurturing, caregiving, and emotional investment in others. This dimension emphasizes the importance of love, empathy, and support in creating a strong emotional foundation.

Key Aspects of Maternal Wealth:

- **Family and Relationships:** Building meaningful and supportive bonds with loved ones.
- **Legacy of Care:** Passing on values, traditions, and emotional strength to future generations.
- **Emotional Security:** Cultivating a sense of safety and trust within relationships.

Maternal Wealth Matters

Maternal wealth fosters resilience and emotional well-being. It strengthens bonds that provide comfort during life's challenges and joy during its triumphs. For parents, it represents the nurturing of children with love, wisdom, and care. For individuals, it extends to friendships, community ties, and acts of kindness.

In this workbook, you will:

- Reflect on the key relationships in your life and how they contribute to your well-being.
- Learn how to nurture emotional wealth by investing in love, trust, and understanding.
- Explore ways to create a legacy of care that supports and uplifts others.

Spiritual Wealth: The Dimension of Purpose

Spiritual wealth is the wealth of the soul—the sense of meaning, fulfillment, and connection to something greater than oneself. It is deeply personal and can be rooted in religious faith, personal beliefs, or a commitment to higher values. Spiritual wealth enriches life by offering clarity, peace, and direction.

Key Aspects of Spiritual Wealth:

- **Core Values:** Understanding and living in alignment with your beliefs and principles.
- **Purpose and Fulfillment:** Finding meaning in your actions and contributions to the world.

- **Mindfulness and Inner Peace:** Cultivating practices that nurture mental clarity and spiritual growth.

Why Spiritual Wealth Matters

Spiritual wealth provides a compass for navigating life's complexities. It helps you remain grounded in your values, find peace amidst chaos, and connect with a deeper sense of purpose. Whether expressed through religious faith, meditation, or acts of service, spiritual wealth is a vital dimension of holistic abundance.

In this workbook, you will:

- Identify your core values and reflect on how they guide your life.
- Practice mindfulness exercises to deepen your connection with the present moment.
- Explore ways to contribute to your community and leave a meaningful legacy.

Financial Wealth: The Dimension of Empowerment

Financial wealth represents the tangible resources that provide stability, security, and opportunities. While it is often equated with material success, financial wealth is about more than accumulating money; it is about using those resources to support your goals, values, and aspirations.

Key Aspects of Financial Wealth:

- **Financial Literacy:** Understanding how to manage, save, and invest money effectively.
- **Stability and Freedom:** Building a financial foundation that allows you to pursue your dreams.
- **Generational Impact:** Creating a legacy of financial knowledge and resources for future generations.

Financial Wealth Matters

Financial wealth empowers you to make choices that align with your values and goals. It provides the freedom to support loved ones, invest in personal growth, and contribute to causes you care about. Without financial stability, other dimensions of wealth can be harder to maintain.

In this workbook, you will:

- Set clear financial goals and create actionable plans to achieve them.
- ____
- ____
- ____
- Learn strategies for managing and investing money wisely.
- ____
- ____
- Reflect on the role of financial wealth in supporting your broader vision of success.

The Interconnection of the Dimensions

While each dimension of wealth is distinct, they are deeply interconnected. A life rich in one dimension but lacking in others is unbalanced and unsustainable. For example:

- Maternal wealth without financial stability can lead to stress and strained relationships.
- Spiritual wealth without emotional connections can feel isolated and ungrounded.
- Financial wealth without spiritual or emotional grounding can feel hollow and unfulfilling.

By cultivating all three dimensions, you create a life that is not only prosperous but also deeply rewarding. This workbook encourages you to explore these intersections and align your actions with your values.

Who Is This Workbook For?

This workbook is for anyone seeking a life of balance and abundance. Whether you are a parent striving to leave a legacy for your children, a professional aiming for financial independence, or a seeker exploring spiritual fulfillment, this guide is designed to meet you where you are.

It is also for:

- Those recovering from financial or emotional setbacks.
- Individuals seeking greater meaning and purpose in their lives.

- Families that are looking to strengthen their bonds and create a shared vision of success.

How to Use This Workbook

This workbook is structured to guide you through the exploration of each dimension of wealth. It includes reflective exercises, practical tools, and actionable strategies to help you build and balance your wealth.

Tips for Success:

1. **Take Your Time:** Each dimension deserves thoughtful reflection. Progress at your own pace.
2. **Be Honest:** Honest self-assessment is key to meaningful growth.
3. **Engage Loved Ones:** Share your journey with family and trusted friends to deepen connections and accountability.
4. **Revisit and Revise:** Wealth is dynamic. Revisit the workbook periodically to reflect on your progress and adjust your goals.

A Legacy of Holistic Wealth

True wealth is not measured in dollars or possessions but in the richness of your relationships, the depth of your purpose, and the security of your resources. The 3 Dimensions of Wealth Workbook invites you to embrace a broader, more meaningful definition of success. By cultivating maternal, spiritual, and financial wealth, you can create a legacy of abundance that enriches your life and inspires those around you.

This journey is about more than achieving goals; it is about transforming your mindset, aligning with your values, and living a life of intentional prosperity. Let this workbook be your guide to unlocking the full potential of the 3 Dimensions of Wealth.

Welcome to your journey of growth, balance, and fulfillment.

Objective: Understand the concept of multidimensional wealth and how it can transform your life.

1. **Definition of Wealth:**
    - Write down your current definition of wealth.
    - ______________________________________
    - How does this definition shape your decisions?
    - ______________________________________
2. **Three Dimensions:**
    - Financial: Income, savings, and investments.
    - Emotional: Relationships, mental health, and self-awareness.
    - Spiritual: Purpose, fulfillment, and connection to a higher power.

Activity: Reflect on how balanced your dimensions are currently. Rate each from 1 (low) to 10 (high). Answer _______________

Maternal Wealth

The Foundation of Emotional Prosperity

Maternal wealth is a profound dimension of prosperity rooted in the nurturing bonds, emotional support, and legacies of care that define our relationships with loved ones. Though the term "maternal" often suggests motherhood, maternal wealth extends beyond biological connections, encompassing all forms of nurturing relationships that provide emotional strength, security, and well-being. This wealth is foundational, influencing how individuals build resilience, navigate challenges, and experience joy and fulfillment.

This chapter explores the importance of maternal wealth, its impact on individuals and families, and how it shapes society. It also includes a worksheet to help you identify the key benefits of maternal wealth in your life.

Understanding Maternal Wealth

Maternal wealth is the emotional and relational capital that stems from nurturing relationships. It is built on love, trust, empathy, and support, and it manifests in the care we receive and offer to others. While it often originates from parental figures, maternal wealth is also cultivated through friendships, mentorships, and community ties.

This dimension of wealth is not measured in dollars or possessions but in the quality of human connections. It influences every aspect of life, from emotional stability to physical health and career success. People with strong maternal wealth often display greater resilience, self-confidence, and a sense of purpose.

The Importance of Material Wealth

1. Emotional Stability and Resilience

Maternal wealth provides a safety net of emotional stability. Knowing that someone cares for you and believes in your potential can be a powerful source of strength. Whether it's a parent, mentor, or friend, nurturing relationships give individuals the confidence to face challenges and recover from setbacks.

- **Example:** A child with a supportive parent or guardian learns to navigate difficult situations with greater ease, developing problem-solving skills and emotional resilience.

2. Strengthening Family Bonds

Families are the cornerstone of society, and maternal wealth plays a crucial role in fostering strong familial relationships. Acts of care, communication, and shared traditions strengthen the bonds that hold families together, creating a sense of belonging and continuity.

- **Example:** Family meals, holiday traditions, and open communication build trust and understanding among family members, ensuring a supportive environment for all.

3. Intergenerational Impact

Maternal wealth is a legacy passed from one generation to the next. The values, traditions, and emotional support imparted by one generation shape the character and success of the next. This intergenerational wealth creates a ripple effect, influencing entire communities.

- **Example:** A parent who emphasizes education and emotional intelligence equips their children with tools for success, who, in turn, pass these values to their own children.

4. Enhancing Mental and Physical Health

Nurturing relationships have a significant impact on mental and physical health. Studies show that individuals with strong social support systems are less likely to experience depression, anxiety, and stress. They also tend to have lower blood pressure, improved immune function, and longer lifespans.

- **Example:** A supportive spouse or friend can encourage healthy habits, such as regular exercise and proper nutrition, contributing to overall well-being.

5. Encouraging Personal Growth

Maternal wealth fosters personal growth by providing a foundation of unconditional love and encouragement. People who feel supported are more likely to take risks, pursue their passions, and achieve their goals.

- **Example:** A mentor's guidance can inspire a young professional to explore new opportunities and build a fulfilling career.

6. Creating a Sense of Community

Maternal wealth extends beyond individual relationships to encompass community connections. Nurturing communities' foster collaboration, mutual aid, and a shared sense of purpose, enhancing social cohesion and collective well-being.

- **Example:** Religious groups, neighborhood associations, and support networks provide emotional and practical assistance, enriching the lives of their members.

The Role of Maternal Wealth in Society

Maternal wealth is not only essential for individual and family well-being but also plays a vital role in societal development. Communities and societies with strong nurturing networks tend to exhibit higher levels of trust, cooperation, and social capital. Conversely, the absence of maternal wealth can lead to social fragmentation, isolation, and conflict.

By investing in maternal wealth—through education, mentorship, and community-building initiatives—societies can create environments that nurture emotional well-being, foster resilience, and promote shared prosperity.

Cultivating Maternal Wealth

Maternal wealth is not static; it requires ongoing effort and intentionality to build and maintain. Here are practical steps to cultivate maternal wealth in your life:

1. Nurture Your Relationships

Invest time and energy in your relationships. Show appreciation, practice active listening, and create opportunities for connection.

2. Be a Source of Support

Offer your time, resources, or a listening ear to those in need. Acts of kindness strengthen bonds and create a sense of reciprocity.

3. Pass on Values and Traditions

Share your values, stories, and traditions with loved ones to create a sense of continuity and purpose.

4. Build a Supportive Network

Surround yourself with people who uplift and inspire you. Join community groups or seek out mentors who align with your values.

5. Practice Self-Care

Maternal wealth begins with self-love. Taking care of your own physical and emotional health enables you to be present for others.

Worksheet: Key Benefits of Maternal Wealth

Use the following worksheet to reflect on the role of maternal wealth in your life and identify its key benefits.

Part 1: Reflecting on Relationships

1. List three people who provide you with emotional support:
    - ______________________________
    - ______________________________
    - ______________________________
2. Describe one way each person has positively impacted your life:
    - ______________________________
    - ______________________________
    - ______________________________

Part 2: Benefits of Maternal Wealth

1. What are the top three benefits of maternal wealth in your life?
    - ______________________________
    - ______________________________
    - ______________________________
2. How have these benefits influenced your personal growth and well-being?
    - ______________________________
    - ______________________________

Part 3: Cultivating Maternal Wealth

1. Identify one relationship you would like to strengthen:
   - ______________________________
2. List three actions you can take to nurture this relationship:
   - ______________________________
   - ______________________________
   - ______________________________
3. What values or traditions do you want to pass on to future generations?
   - ______________________________
   - ______________________________

Conclusion

Maternal wealth is a cornerstone of a fulfilling and prosperous life. It provides the emotional foundation needed to navigate challenges, achieve personal growth, and foster meaningful relationships. By recognizing its importance and actively cultivating it, you can create a legacy of love, care, and resilience that enriches not only your own life but also the lives of those around you.

This dimension of wealth reminds us that prosperity is not measured in material terms alone but in the quality of our connections and the impact we have on others. Through the reflections and actions prompted by this workbook, you can harness the transformative power of maternal wealth and make it an integral part of your journey to holistic abundance.

INSURANCE A MUST HAVE

The Importance of Health Insurance and Life Insurance

Insurance plays a vital role in safeguarding individuals and families from unforeseen financial burdens and ensuring long-term security. Among the various types of insurance, health insurance and life insurance are two of the most crucial. Health insurance protects against medical expenses, while life insurance provides financial security to loved ones in the event of one's untimely death. Together, these forms of insurance form the foundation of a comprehensive financial plan, offering peace of mind and stability.

This chapter delves into the importance of health and life insurance, their key benefits, and how they contribute to financial well-being. Worksheets for each type of insurance are included to help you plan and manage your coverage effectively.

Health Insurance: A Pillar of Financial and Physical Security

Matthew 7:24-25 KJV

24 Therefore whosoever heareth these sayings of mine, and doeth them, I will liken him unto a wise man, which built his house upon a rock: 25 And the rain descended, and the floods came, and the winds blew, and beat upon that house; and it fell not: for it was founded upon a rock.

What is Health Insurance?

Health insurance is a contract between an individual and an insurance company that provides financial coverage for medical expenses. It covers a wide range of healthcare needs, including doctor visits, hospital stays, surgeries, medications, and preventive care.

Why Health Insurance is Essential

1. **Protection Against High Medical costs:** Healthcare expenses can be overwhelming, especially for serious illnesses or emergencies. Health insurance acts as a financial buffer, covering a significant portion of these costs and preventing individuals from depleting their savings.

- **Example:** A single hospital stay can cost thousands of dollars, but with health insurance, out-of-pocket expenses are significantly reduced.

2. **Access to Quality Healthcare:** Having health insurance ensures timely access to medical services. It allows individuals to consult specialists, undergo diagnostic tests, and receive treatments without delay, improving health outcomes.

- **Example:** Preventive services, like vaccinations and screenings, are often covered at no cost, helping to detect and manage conditions early.

3. **Encourages Preventive Care:** Many health insurance plans prioritize preventive care, encouraging policyholders to stay proactive about their health. Regular check-ups and screenings can detect issues early, reducing the need for costly treatments later.
4. **Covers Chronic and Pre-existing Conditions:** Modern health insurance plans often cover chronic diseases and pre-existing conditions, ensuring that individuals with ongoing health needs receive the care they require.
5. **Employer and Government Support:** In many countries, health insurance is provided or subsidized by employers or governments, making it more accessible and affordable.

Types of Health Insurance

- **Individual Plans:** Purchased directly by individuals to cover themselves and their families.

- **Employer-Sponsored Plans:** Provided by employers as part of employee benefits.
- **Government Plans:** Offered by governments, such as Medicare, Medicaid, or national healthcare systems.
- **Supplemental Insurance:** Covers additional costs not included in primary plans, such as dental or vision care.

Life Insurance

Securing Your Loved Ones' Future

What is Life Insurance?

Life insurance is a contract between an individual (policyholder) and an insurance company, where the insurer pays a lump sum to the designated beneficiaries upon the policyholder's death. This financial safety net ensures that loved ones are protected from financial hardship in the policyholder's absence.

Why Life Insurance is Essential

1. **Financial Protection for Dependents:** Life insurance provides a safety net for family members, ensuring they can maintain their standard of living even in the absence of the primary breadwinner.

- **Example:** Life insurance payouts can cover daily expenses, mortgage payments, education costs, and other financial obligations.

2. **Pays Off Debts:** In the event of the policyholder's death, life insurance can settle outstanding debts, such as loans, credit cards, or mortgages, preventing the burden from falling on surviving family members.
3. **Covers Funeral and End-of-Life Expenses:** Life insurance helps cover the costs associated with funerals, which can be significant. This relieves the family of additional financial stress during an emotional time.
4. **Builds Generational Wealth:** Certain types of life insurance policies, such as whole life or universal life insurance, include a cash value component. This can be used to build wealth over time and passed on to heirs.
5. **Supports Long-Term Financial Goals:** Life insurance can be used as part of a long-term financial strategy, providing funds for children's education, retirement, or even charitable contributions.

Types of Life Insurance

- **Term Life Insurance:** Provides coverage for a specific period, such as 10, 20, or 30 years. It is typically more affordable and straightforward.
- **Whole Life Insurance:** Offers lifelong coverage and includes a cash value component that grows over time.
- **Universal Life Insurance:** Combines lifelong coverage with flexible premiums and a cash value component tied to market performance.
- **Group Life Insurance:** Offered by employers as part of employee benefits, often with limited coverage.

Health Insurance Worksheet

Part 1: Current Health Insurance Plan

1. Do you currently have health insurance? (Yes/No): ____________________
2. Provider Name: ____
3. Type of Plan (Individual, Employer-Sponsored, Government):

   ____

4. Coverage Details:
   - Primary Care Visits:

     ____

   - Specialist Visits:

     ____

   - Medications:

     ____

   - Preventive Services: _____________________________________

Part 2: Evaluating Your Coverage

1. Are there any services or treatments you feel are missing from your coverage? (Yes/No): ____________________
   - If yes, what are they? ____
2. Do you feel your premiums and deductibles are affordable? (Yes/No):

   ____

   - If no, what adjustments are needed? ____________________________
3. How often do you use your health insurance for medical care? (Rarely/Often):

   ____

Part 3: Future Health Insurance Needs

1. Are you planning any major medical procedures or family changes (e.g., childbirth, surgery)? (Yes/No): ___________
   - If yes, what are they? ______________________________________
2. Would you benefit from supplemental insurance (e.g., dental, vision)? (Yes/No): ___________
3. List any steps to improve or update your health insurance:
   - ____
   - ____

Life Insurance Worksheet

Part 1: Current Life Insurance Plan

1. Do you currently have life insurance? (Yes/No): ___________________
2. Provider Name: ____
3. Type of Policy (Term, Whole, Universal): __________________________
4. Coverage Amount: ____
5. Monthly Premium: ____

Part 2: Beneficiaries

1. List your primary beneficiaries:
   - Name: _______________ Relationship: _______% ____

- Name: ________________ Relationship: _______ %____
- Name: ________________ Relationship: _______ %____

2. List your contingent beneficiaries (if primary beneficiaries are unavailable):
    - Name: ________________ Relationship: ________ %___
    - Name: ________________ Relationship: ________ %___

Part 3: Evaluating Your Coverage

1. Is your coverage amount sufficient to meet your family's needs? (Yes/No): _________
    - If no, how much additional coverage do you need? ______________
2. Do you have any outstanding debts that life insurance should cover? (Yes/No): _________
    - If yes, what are they? ____
    - ____
    - ____
3. Are there specific goals you want your policy to support (e.g., education, retirement)? (Yes/No): _________
    - If yes, what are they? ____
    - ____
    - ____

Part 4: Updating Your Plan

1. Do you need to adjust your beneficiaries or coverage? (Yes/No): ___________
    - If yes, what changes are needed? _______________________________
2. List any steps to update or improve your life insurance:
    - _______________________________
    - _______________________________

Conclusion

Health insurance and life insurance are indispensable tools for financial security and peace of mind. Health insurance protects against the rising costs of medical care, ensuring access to quality services and reducing financial stress. Life insurance secures the future of loved ones, providing a safety net that supports their needs and goals.

By understanding the importance of these insurance types and actively managing your coverage, you can create a comprehensive safety net for yourself and your family. Use the worksheets provided to assess your current plans, identify areas for improvement, and take actionable steps toward better coverage and protection. In doing so, you'll be investing in both your present well-being and your legacy for the future.

LEGAL SERVICE MATTERS

The Importance of Having a Lawyer Safeguarding Your Rights and Interests

Legal issues, whether personal or professional, can be complex and challenging to navigate without expert guidance. Having a lawyer or legal counsel ensures that your rights are protected, your interests are prioritized, and you are equipped to make informed decisions in legal matters. From drafting contracts and settling disputes to representing you in court, a lawyer is an invaluable ally in today's litigious and regulated world.

This chapter explores the importance of having a lawyer, highlights three trusted organizations that provide legal services, and includes a worksheet to help you evaluate your legal needs.

Why Having a Lawyer is Crucial

1. Legal Expertise

Lawyers have specialized knowledge and training in the law, enabling them to understand complex legal issues and procedures. Whether it's interpreting contracts, navigating tax laws, or defending against criminal charges, their expertise is invaluable.

- **Example:** If you are purchasing property, a lawyer can review contracts, ensure compliance with zoning laws, and address any disputes that arise during the process.

2. Protecting Your Rights

A lawyer acts as your advocate, ensuring your rights are upheld in any legal matter. Whether you are entering into a business agreement or defending yourself in court, their primary duty is to protect your interests.

- **Example:** In a workplace dispute, a lawyer can help you understand your rights, negotiate settlements, or take your case to court if necessary.

3. Mitigating Risks

Legal issues can have significant financial, professional, and personal consequences. Having a lawyer reduces the risk of making mistakes that could lead to lawsuits, penalties, or other adverse outcomes.

- **Example:** Entrepreneurs rely on lawyers to establish their businesses, ensuring compliance with regulations and safeguarding against potential liabilities.

4. Navigating Complex Legal Processes

Legal procedures, from filing documents to appearing in court, can be daunting. Lawyers are well-versed in these processes, ensuring they are completed efficiently and correctly.

- **Example:** In estate planning, a lawyer can draft wills, trusts, and other documents to ensure your assets are distributed according to your wishes.

5. Conflict Resolution

Lawyers are skilled in negotiation, mediation, and litigation, making them essential for resolving disputes. Whether it's a business disagreement, divorce, or landlord-tenant issue, a lawyer can help find the best solution.

- **Example:** In a family dispute over inheritance, a lawyer can mediate discussions and, if necessary, represent your interests in court.

6. Strategic Guidance

A lawyer provides strategic advice tailored to your specific situation. They consider the legal, financial, and personal aspects of your case, helping you make decisions that align with your goals.

- **Example:** A corporate lawyer might advise a company on structuring a merger or acquisition to minimize risks and maximize benefits.

Three Best Organizations That Provide Legal Services

Selecting a trusted legal service provider is crucial for receiving competent and reliable assistance. Below are three reputable organizations offering legal services:

1. LegalShield

- **Overview:** LegalShield provides affordable legal services to individuals and businesses through a subscription-based model. Members gain access to a network of attorneys for advice, document review, and representation.
- **Services Offered:**
  - Consultation on personal and business legal matters.
  - Document preparation and review.
  - Representation for traffic violations and civil cases.
- **Ideal For:** Individuals and small businesses seeking affordable, ongoing legal support.

2. American Bar Association (ABA)

- **Overview:** The ABA is a professional organization for lawyers in the United States. It provides resources to both attorneys and the public, including lawyer referral services.
- **Services Offered:**
  - Lawyer referral programs connecting individuals with qualified attorneys.

    - Public legal education resources.
    - Advocacy for legal rights and access to justice.
- **Ideal For:** Individuals looking for reputable, experienced lawyers in specific legal fields.

3. Legal Aid Society

- **Overview:** The Legal Aid Society offers free or low-cost legal services to those who cannot afford private representation. They focus on cases involving basic human needs, such as housing, employment, and family law.
- **Services Offered:**
    - Representation in civil, criminal, and family law cases.
    - Assistance with housing disputes, employment rights, and public bcncfits.
    - Advocacy for marginalized and underserved communities.
- **Ideal For:** Low-income individuals and families requiring legal assistance.

How to Choose the Right Lawyer

Selecting the right lawyer depends on your specific legal needs, budget, and personal preferences. Consider the following when choosing a lawyer:

- **Specialization:** Ensure the lawyer has expertise in the area of law relevant to your case.
- **Experience:** Look for a lawyer with a proven track record in similar cases.

- **Reputation:** Check reviews, references, and professional affiliations.
- **Cost:** Understand the lawyer's fee structure and ensure it aligns with your budget.
- **Communication:** Choose a lawyer who communicates clearly and keeps you informed.

Worksheet: Assessing Your Legal Needs

Part 1: Current Legal Needs

1. What legal issues are you currently facing?
    - ______________________________
    - ______________________________
    - ______________________________
2. Do you require a lawyer for a one-time issue or ongoing support?
    - ______________________________
3. Which area of law does your issue fall under? (e.g., family, business, criminal)
    - ______________________________

Part 2: Evaluating Lawyer Options

1. Have you identified potential lawyers or organizations? (Yes/No): __________
    - If yes, list them below:
        - ______________________________
        - ______________________________
        - ______________________________
2. What criteria are most important to you when selecting a lawyer?
    - ______________________________
    - ______________________________
3. Have you researched their specialization, experience, and reputation? (Yes/No): __________

Part 3: Beneficiary and Representation Details

1. Who would benefit from resolving this legal issue (e.g., family, business)?
   - ______________________________
2. If applicable, list any individuals or entities you need to name as beneficiaries or involved parties:
   - ______________________________
   - ______________________________

Part 4: Budgeting for Legal Services

1. What is your budget for legal services?
   - ______________________________
2. Have you discussed payment terms with potential lawyers? (Yes/No): __________
3. Are you eligible for free or subsidized legal services? (Yes/No): __________

Part 5: Next Steps

1. What steps will you take to secure legal representation?
   - ______________________________
   - ______________________________
   - ______________________________
2. How will you prepare for your first meeting with the lawyer?
   - ______________________________
   - ______________________________

Conclusion

Having a lawyer is not just about addressing legal issues; it's about proactively safeguarding your rights, interests, and future. Whether navigating personal matters, managing a business, or dealing with unexpected challenges, legal counsel provides expertise, guidance, and peace of mind.

Organizations like LegalShield, the American Bar Association, and the Legal Aid Society make legal services accessible to individuals from all walks of life. By assessing your needs and leveraging trusted resources, you can ensure that you are well-prepared to handle any legal challenges that come your way.

The included worksheet is designed to help you reflect on your current legal needs, evaluate potential options, and take actionable steps toward securing the right representation. With the support of a competent lawyer, you can face legal issues confidently and achieve the best possible outcomes.

Financial Dimension

Objective: Build a solid foundation of financial literacy and security.

1. **Financial Goals:**
   - Short-term (1 year): ___________________________
   - Mid-term (5 years): ___________________________
   - Long-term (10+ years): ___________________________
2. **Budgeting:**
   - Track your monthly income and expenses.
   - Identify areas to save or invest.

Activity: Create a sample budget for one month using the table provided.

3. **Investments:**
   - Understand the basics of stocks, bonds, and mutual funds.
   - Research one investment option and write a short summary.

Emotional Dimension

Objective: Cultivate emotional resilience and meaningful connections.

Relationship Health:

- List the five people you spend the most time with. Do they uplift you?
- 1. ______________________________
- 2. ______________________________
- 3. ___________________________
- 4. _______________________________
- 5. _______________________________
- What changes can you make to improve your emotional environment?
- 1. ________________________________
- 2. ________________________________
- 3. ________________________________

Self-Care Practices:

- Identify activities that rccharge you (e.g., exercise, meditation).
- 1. ________________________________
- 2. ________________________________
- Commit to practicing one self-care activity daily for 30 days.
- 1. ________________________________

Activity: Write a gratitude journal entry each day for a week.

Emotional Triggers:

- Identify three common triggers.
- 1. ____________________________________
- 2. ____________________________________

- 3. ____
- Develop a coping strategy for each.
- 1. ____
- 2. ____
- 3. ____

Spiritual Dimension

Objective: Deepen your sense of purpose and connection.

Identifying Purpose:

- What are your core values?
- 1. ____
- 2. ____
- 3. ____
- How do these values align with your daily actions?
- 1. ____
- 2. ____

Mindfulness and Meditation:

- Practice a 5-minute meditation focusing on your breath.
- Write down how you feel before and after the meditation.
- 1. ____

- 2. ____

Service to Others:

- Plan one act of kindness this week.
- ____
- Reflect on how it made you feel and the impact on others.
- ____

Goal-Setting Worksheets

SMART Goals Template:

- Specific: What exactly do you want to achieve?
- ____
- Measurable: How will you know you've achieved it?
- ____
- Achievable: Is it realistic? Y/N
- Relevant: Does it align with your values and priorities? Y/N
- Time-bound: What is your deadline? ________________

Activity: Fill out the SMART goals worksheet for one goal in each dimension.

Tracking Your Progress

1. **Weekly Check-Ins:**
    - Reflect on your achievements and challenges.
    - ____________________________________
    - Adjust your strategies as needed.
    - ____________________________________

Monthly Review:

- Use the provided table to track financial, emotional, and spiritual milestones.

Activity: Set aside 30 minutes each month to review your progress.

Reflection Exercises

Journaling Prompts:

- What did I learn about myself this week?
- ____________________________________
- What challenges did I face, and how did I overcome them?
- ____________________________________
- ____________________________________
- How can I improve next week?
- ____________________________________

Vision Board Creation:

- Gather images and words that represent your goals.
- Create a vision board and place it where you'll see it daily.

Resources and Next Steps

1. **Books and Articles:**
   - Recommended reading list to deepen your understanding of wealth dimensions.
2. **Mentorship and Community:**
   - Join groups or find a mentor to support your journey.
3. **Commitment Contract:**
   - Write a contract to yourself, committing to this journey of multidimensional wealth.

Activity: Sign and date your commitment contract.

Financial Dimension

Objective: Build a solid foundation of financial literacy and security.

1. **Emergency Contact Information:**
   - Name: ______________________________
   - Relationship: ______________________________
   - Phone Number: ______________________________
   - Email Address: ______________________________
2. **Beneficiary Information:**

- Name: ____________________________
- Relationship: ____________________________
- Contact Information: ____________________________
- Details of Financial or Property Assignment: ____________________________

3. **Financial Goals:**
   - Short-term (1 year): ____________________________
   - Mid-term (5 years): ____________________________
   - Long-term (10+ years): ____________________________
4. **Chart of Financial Institutions,**
5. Real Estate ____

   Value $ ________________________________
6. Valuables: ___________________________________

   Projected Value $_________________________

   Financial Institutions

   - ___________________________ Value $ ___________
   - ___________________________ Value $ ___________
   - ___________________________ Value $ ___________
7. **Budgeting:**
   - Track your monthly income and expenses.
   - Income $ ____________________
   - Expense $ ___________________
   - Identify areas to save or invest.

- ______________________________
- ______________________________
- ______________________________

Activity: Create a sample budget for one month using the table provided.

6. **Investments:**
    - Understand the basics of stocks, bonds, and mutual funds.
    - Research one investment option and write a short summary.

Emotional Dimension

Objective: Cultivate emotional resilience and meaningful connections.

1. **Relationship Health:**
    - List the two people you spend the most time with.
    - 1. ______________________________
    - 2. ______________________________
    - 3. ______________________________
    - 4. ______________________________
    - 5. ______________________________
    - What changes can you make to improve your emotional environment?
    - 1. ______________________________
    - 2. ______________________________
    - 3. ______________________________
2. **Self-Care Practices:**
    - Identify activities that recharge you (e.g., exercise, meditation, prayer).

- ______________________________________
- Commit to practicing spiritual growth activity daily for 30 days.
- ____________________________________
- ____________________________________
- ____________________________________

Activity: Write a gratitude journal entry each day for a week.

3. **Emotional Triggers:**
    - Identify three common triggers.
    - ___________________________________
    - ___________________________________
    - ___________________________________
    - Develop a coping strategy for each.
    - ___________________________________
    - ___________________________________
    - ___________________________________

PRAYER WORKSHEET

Personal Prayer Request Worksheet

1. Personal Prayer Focus

- What area of your life are you focusing on in prayer? (e.g., family, career, health, spiritual growth)

____

____

2. Specific Prayer Requests

- Write down specific requests for this focus area:
  1. ________________________________
  2. ________________________________
  3. ________________________________

3. Scriptures to Guide Your Prayer

- Choose or write down Bible verses that align with your prayer requests:
  1. ________________________________
  2. ________________________________

4. Gratitude and Thanksgiving

- List three things you are thankful for in this area of your life:
  1. ________________________________
  2. ________________________________
  3. ________________________________

5. Reflections and Updates

- Reflect on how God is responding to your prayers or providing guidance:

  ____

  ____

6. Prayer Journal Entry

- Write a short prayer to God, including your requests, thanksgiving, and reflections:

  ____

  ____

  ____

____

Tips for Using This Worksheet

1. Review and update your prayer requests regularly.
2. Take time to reflect on God's responses and express gratitude for His faithfulness.
3. Share your requests with trusted prayer partners or groups if you feel comfortable.

This worksheet will help you cultivate a deeper, more intentional prayer life while building your faith and gratitude for God's work in your life.

FINANCIAL DIMENSION

CRYPTO CURRENCY

The Digital Revolution in Wealth – Crypto Currency

Cryptocurrency represents one of the most significant advancements in financial technology in the 21st century. Emerging from the revolutionary idea of decentralized digital money, cryptocurrencies have transformed the way people think about wealth, investment, and financial freedom. With Bitcoin's inception in 2009, the concept of a peer-to-peer currency without the need for intermediaries like banks and governments became a reality. Today, cryptocurrencies are not just digital coins but an entire ecosystem of innovation, including smart contracts, decentralized finance (DeFi), and non-fungible tokens (NFTs).

This chapter explores the fundamentals of cryptocurrency, its benefits and risks, trusted platforms for investment, and common scams associated with this technology. A worksheet is also included to help readers reflect on their understanding of cryptocurrency and prepare for investing wisely.

Understanding Cryptocurrency

What is Cryptocurrency?

A cryptocurrency is a digital or virtual currency that uses cryptography for security. Unlike traditional currencies issued by governments, cryptocurrencies operate on decentralized networks using blockchain technology—a distributed ledger that records all transactions across multiple computers.

Key characteristics of cryptocurrencies include:

- **Decentralization:** No central authority governs cryptocurrencies.
- **Transparency:** All transactions are recorded on a public ledger.
- **Security:** Cryptographic algorithms ensure the integrity and security of transactions.
- **Global Accessibility:**

Types of Cryptocurrencies

Cryptocurrencies can be sent and received anywhere in the world without intermediaries.

Cryptocurrencies come in various forms, each serving unique purposes. Some of the most well-known types include:

1. **Bitcoin (BTC):** The first and most recognized cryptocurrency, often referred to as "digital gold."

2. **Ethereum (ETH):** A platform for decentralized applications (DApps) and smart contracts.
3. **Tether (USDT):** A stablecoin pegged to the value of fiat currencies like the U.S. dollar.
4. **Binance Coin (BNB):** Used on the Binance exchange for trading and transaction fees.
5. **Cardano (ADA):** Known for its focus on scalability, security, and sustainability.

Benefits of Cryptocurrency

1. **Financial Freedom:** Cryptocurrencies offer an alternative to traditional financial systems, enabling users to control their money without reliance on banks or governments. This democratization of finance provides greater access to people in underbanked regions.
2. **Low Transaction Costs:** Compared to traditional financial systems, cryptocurrency transactions often have lower fees, especially for cross-border payments.
3. **Investment Opportunities:** The volatility of cryptocurrencies presents significant opportunities for investment. Early adopters of Bitcoin, Ethereum, and other assets have experienced remarkable returns on their investments.
4. **Decentralized Finance (DeFi):** Cryptocurrencies power DeFi applications, allowing users to borrow, lend, and earn interest on their holdings without intermediaries.

5. **Security and Transparency:** Blockchain technology ensures that transactions are secure, immutable, and transparent, reducing the risk of fraud.

Risks of Cryptocurrency

1. **Volatility:** Cryptocurrencies are known for their price volatility, which can lead to significant gains or losses.
2. **Regulatory Uncertainty:** Governments worldwide are still determining how to regulate cryptocurrencies, leading to potential legal and tax complications.
3. **Hacking and Scams:** While blockchain technology is secure, exchanges and wallets can be vulnerable to hacks. Additionally, the anonymity of cryptocurrency transactions has made it a target for scams.
4. **Lack of Consumer Protection:** Unlike traditional banks, there are limited mechanisms for recovering lost or stolen cryptocurrencies.

Trusted Platforms for Cryptocurrency Investment

Choosing a reliable platform is crucial for safe cryptocurrency investment. Here are three of the most trusted platforms:

1. Coinbase

- **Overview:** Coinbase is one of the most popular cryptocurrency exchanges, especially for beginners. Based in the United States, it offers a user-friendly interface, high security, and a wide range of cryptocurrencies.
- **Features:**
  - Supports major cryptocurrencies like Bitcoin, Ethereum, and Litecoin.
  - Insurance protection for stored assets.
  - Educational resources for new investors.
- **Ideal For:** Beginners seeking a secure and straightforward platform.

2. Binance

- **Overview:** Binance is one of the largest cryptocurrency exchanges in the world, known for its advanced trading features and low fees.
- **Features:**
  - Supports hundreds of cryptocurrencies and trading pairs.
  - Offers staking, futures trading, and margin trading.
  - High liquidity and competitive fees.
- **Ideal For:** Experienced investors and active traders.

3. Kraken

- **Overview:** Kraken is a reputable exchange with a strong focus on security and compliance. It provides a range of features for both beginners and advanced users.

- **Features:**
  - Supports spot trading, futures, and staking.
  - Advanced security measures, including cold storage for assets.
  - Extensive cryptocurrency listings.
- **Ideal For:** Investors looking for a secure platform with diverse trading options.

Cryptocurrency Scams

The rapid rise of cryptocurrencies has also attracted scammers. Here are some common types of cryptocurrency scams:

1. Fake Investment Platforms

Scammers create fake websites or apps that promise high returns on investments. Once victims deposit funds, the scammers disappear.

2. Phishing Scams

Fraudsters send fake emails or messages pretending to be legitimate exchanges or wallets, tricking users into revealing private keys or passwords.

3. Rug Pulls

In DeFi, developers launch a new cryptocurrency, attract investors, and then abandon the project after cashing out, leaving investors with worthless tokens.

4. Ponzi Schemes

Scammers promise high returns to early investors using funds from new investors. These schemes eventually collapse when no new investments are made.

5. Impersonation Scams

Fraudsters impersonate celebrities, influencers, or trusted individuals to solicit cryptocurrency payments.

How to Avoid Cryptocurrency Scams

1. **Do Your Research**

- Verify the legitimacy of platforms, projects, and individuals before investing.
- Read reviews and check for regulatory compliance.

2. **Use Trusted Platforms**

- Stick to well-known and reputable exchanges like Coinbase, Binance, and Kraken.

3. **Secure Your Wallets**

- Use hardware wallets for long-term storage.
- Enable two-factor authentication (2FA) on all accounts.

4. **Be Skeptical of Unrealistic Returns**

- Avoid platforms or schemes promising guaranteed or unusually high returns.

5. **Double-Check Addresses**

- Always confirm wallet addresses before sending funds to avoid phishing attempts.
-

Worksheet: Reflecting on Cryptocurrency

Part 1: Understanding Your Goals

1. Why are you interested in cryptocurrency?
    - ______________________________
    - ______________________________
2. What are your short-term and long-term goals for investing in cryptocurrency?
    - Short-term: ______________________________
    - Long-term: ______________________________

Part 2: Assessing Risk

1. How much are you willing to invest in cryptocurrency relative to your overall portfolio?
    - ______________________________
2. What is your risk tolerance (low, medium, high)?
    - ______________________________
3. What steps will you take to minimize risks?

- ______________________________
- ______________________________

Part 3: Choosing a Platform

1. Which of the three trusted platforms (Coinbase, Binance, Kraken) do you feel most comfortable using, and why?
   - ______________________________
2. What features are most important to you in a cryptocurrency platform?
   - ______________________________
   - ______________________________

Part 4: Avoiding Scams

1. What research steps will you take before investing in a cryptocurrency project?
   - ______________________________
   - ______________________________
2. How will you secure your cryptocurrency holdings?
   - ______________________________
   - ______________________________
3. What signs of scams will you look out for?
   - ______________________________
   - ______________________________

Conclusion

Cryptocurrency is a transformative financial innovation that offers both opportunities and risks. By understanding its fundamentals, benefits, and pitfalls, you can navigate this dynamic space with confidence. Choosing trusted platforms, staying informed, and taking security precautions are essential for successful cryptocurrency investment.

This chapter aims to empower you with the knowledge and tools to make informed decisions, avoid scams, and achieve your financial goals through cryptocurrency. With careful planning and due diligence, cryptocurrency can become a valuable part of your wealth-building journey.

Financial Dimension Continues

Objective: Build a solid foundation of financial literacy and security.

1. **Emergency Contact Information:**
    - Name: ____________________________
    - Relationship: ____________________________
    - Phone Number: ____________________________
    - Email Address: ____________________________
2. **Beneficiary Information:**
    - Name: ____________________________
    - Relationship: ____________________________
    - Contact Information: ____________________________
    - Details of Financial or Property Assignment:

      ____
3. **Power of Attorney (POA):**
    - **General POA:** Grants broad authority to act on your behalf.
    - **Limited POA:** Authorizes specific actions or transactions.
    - **Durable POA:** Remains in effect if you become incapacitated.
    - **Springing POA:** Comes into effect only under specific conditions, such as incapacitation.
    - **Duration:** Specify timeframes or conditions for activation and termination.
4. **Will:**
    - Purpose: Outlines how your assets will be distributed after your death.

- Components: Executor, beneficiaries, guardianship for minors.
- Duration: Valid until formally revoked or replaced.

5. **Pay on Death (POD):**
   - Definition: Allows you to designate a beneficiary to receive funds directly from a bank account upon your death.
   - Benefits: Avoids probate, ensures quick transfer of funds.
6. **Co-Ownership on Bank Accounts:**
   - Types: Joint accounts, survivorship accounts.
   - Considerations: Rights of survivorship, liability for co-owner actions, ease of access.

Updated Additions to Financial Dimension

7. **Starting a New Business:**
   - Research your market and competitors thoroughly.
   - Develop a solid business plan outlining goals, strategies, and financial projections.
   - Register your business legally and set up necessary permits/licenses.
8. **Obtaining Business Funding:**
   - Apply for small business loans through banks or government programs.
   - Seek investors by pitching your business idea with a clear value proposition.
   - Use personal savings or crowdfunding platforms to raise initial capital.
9. **Advertising Your Business:**
   - Leverage social media platforms to reach your target audience.

- Use local and online advertising, such as Google Ads or community boards.
- Offer promotions or referral incentives to attract customers.

10. **Tracking Business Success:**

- Use key performance indicators (KPIs) such as revenue, profit margins, and customer retention rates.
- Collect customer feedback through surveys and reviews to assess satisfaction and areas for improvement.
- Regularly review financial statements and compare them against your business goals.

FINANCIAL SCAM

Common Business Scams:

- Phishing emails pretending to be from legitimate organizations.
- Fake invoices requesting payment for services not rendered.
- Overpayment scams where scammers send a fraudulent check and ask for a refund.

Avoiding Scams:

- Verify the identity of the sender before making any payments or sharing sensitive information.
- Use secure payment methods and avoid paying through untraceable means.

- Educate employees about recognizing and reporting potential scams.

Protecting Your Business from Scams:

- Implement robust cybersecurity measures, including firewalls and antivirus software.
- Regularly review financial records for any discrepancies or unusual activities.
- Establish clear policies for verifying transactions and communications.

Recovering from Scams:

- Report the scam to law enforcement and relevant authorities immediately.
- Contact your financial institution to stop or reverse any fraudulent transactions.
- Conduct a thorough review of your business processes to identify vulnerabilities and prevent future incidents.

Small Business Scams and Their Economic Impact

Small business scams are fraudulent activities targeting small enterprises to exploit their limited resources, less robust security measures, and occasional lack of awareness about sophisticated threats. These scams can take many forms, including phishing attacks, fake invoices, overpayment frauds, and identity theft. The financial and operational consequences of falling victim to such scams can be devastating for small businesses, which often operate with tight budgets and limited cash flow.

Types of Small Business Scams

1. **Phishing Scams:** Fraudsters send deceptive emails or messages pretending to be from legitimate organizations. They aim to steal sensitive information like passwords, banking details, or customer data.
2. **Fake Invoices:** Scammers send invoices for products or services that were never provided. Busy businesses may unknowingly pay these fraudulent invoices.
3. **Overpayment Fraud:** A scammer overpays using a fake check, then requests a refund for the excess amount. The check eventually bounces, and the business loses the refunded amount.
4. **Business Identity Theft:** Criminals steal a business's identity to access its credit or finances. This type of fraud can severely damage a company's creditworthiness.

Economic Impact on Small Businesses

The economic impact of scams on small businesses is often disproportionate compared to larger enterprises due to their limited resources and thinner profit margins. The consequences can range from immediate financial losses to long-term operational challenges.

1. **Direct Financial Losses:** Scams can result in the loss of money, whether through fraudulent transactions, payment for non-existent goods, or stolen

funds. These immediate losses can disrupt cash flow, leading to difficulty in paying employees, vendors, or operating expenses.

2. **Reputational Damage:** A scam that compromises customer data or reveals lapses in a company's security can harm its reputation. Small businesses often rely on trust and customer loyalty and losing that trust can result in reduced sales and long-term revenue loss.
3. **Operational Disruptions:** Recovering from a scam often requires significant time and resources. This includes legal actions, negotiations with financial institutions, and implementing improved security measures. The diversion of resources to address the scam can hinder normal business operations.
4. **Creditworthiness and Financial Health:** Scams involving identity theft or unpaid fraudulent debts can damage a business's credit rating. This can make it harder to secure loans or attract investment, stifling future growth opportunities.
5. **Increased Costs:** Businesses that have experienced scams often need to invest in enhanced security measures, employee training, and fraud detection tools, further straining their financial resources.

Broader Economic Implications

On a larger scale, small business scams can also impact the economy. Small businesses are vital contributors to job creation, local economic activity, and innovation. When these businesses face financial distress due to scams, the ripple effects can be felt across the community. Layoffs, reduced investment, or even business closures can lead to decreased local economic activity and higher unemployment rates.

Additionally, the prevalence of scams erodes overall trust in the marketplace. Customers and businesses may become hesitant to engage in transactions, slowing economic activity. Regulatory bodies may also face increased pressure to intervene, leading to higher compliance costs for all businesses.

Conclusion

Small business scams pose a significant threat not only to individual businesses but also to the broader economy. Awareness, vigilance, and investment in preventive measures are critical for safeguarding businesses from these fraudulent activities. By recognizing the types of scams and their potential impact, small business owners can better protect their operations and contribute to a more secure and thriving economy.

PERSONAL ELECTRONIC DEVICE

Cell Phone Protection and the Importance of Granting Access to a Trusted Person

Cell phones have become essential tools in modern life, storing vast amounts of personal and sensitive information. From banking details and passwords to personal photos and important documents, cell phones act as digital vaults. While we rely heavily on our phones for convenience, many people overlook the critical need to ensure that a trusted person has access in the event of untimely death or incapacitation. Without proper planning, this vital information may be lost forever, causing complications for loved ones and potentially hindering important legal or financial processes.

This comprehensive guide explores strategies for protecting your cell phone, the importance of granting access to a trusted individual, and how to prepare for unforeseen circumstances.

The Critical Role of Cell Phones in Modern Life

Cell phones are no longer just communication devices; they are multi-functional tools that store a wide range of data. Below are some of the most critical types of information stored on phones:

1. **Financial Data:** Banking apps, cryptocurrency wallets, payment apps (like PayPal and Venmo), and credit card details.
2. **Personal Identity Information:** Photos of IDs, passports, Social Security numbers, and medical records.
3. **Communication Records:** Emails, text messages, and call logs, which may contain sensitive or valuable information.
4. **Memories and Media:** Photos, videos, and voice recordings that are irreplaceable.
5. **Passwords and Login Credentials:** Many people use password managers or save login details directly on their devices.
6. **Legal and Business Documents:** Contracts, agreements, and other critical files often stored in cloud services linked to phones.

The loss of access to this information can have far-reaching consequences, both emotional and practical, for loved ones.

The Risks of Not Granting Access

Failing to plan for access to your phone in the event of your untimely death or incapacitation can lead to numerous challenges, including:

1. **Legal and Financial Hurdles:** Loved ones may face difficulties accessing accounts or settling financial matters, such as closing bank accounts or managing investments.
2. **Missed Opportunities:** Time-sensitive actions, such as responding to legal notices or paying bills, may be missed.

3. **Loss of Sentimental Value:** Personal photos and videos that hold sentimental value may be permanently lost.
4. **Data Breaches:** Without proper planning, unauthorized individuals might exploit the lack of oversight to gain access.

Granting Access to a Trusted Person

To ensure your digital legacy is preserved and your loved ones can manage your affairs effectively, granting access to a trusted person is essential. Here's how to do it:

1. Choose a Trusted Individual

Select someone who is reliable, responsible, and capable of handling sensitive information. This person should understand the importance of confidentiality and respect your privacy.

2. Use Digital Legacy Tools

Many companies now offer tools to grant posthumous access to accounts:

- **Apple's Digital Legacy Program:** Allows users to designate a legacy contact to access data on their Apple devices.
- **Google's Inactive Account Manager:** Enables users to specify a trusted person who can access their account after a period of inactivity.

3. Share Access Securely

- Provide your trusted person with your phone's unlock PIN, pattern, or password.
- Use a secure method, such as a password manager, to share login credentials for key apps and services.

4. Store Backup Data

- Regularly back up your phone's data to cloud services or an external hard drive.
- Ensure your trusted person knows where to find the backup and how to access it.

5. Document Instructions

Create a clear document outlining:

- The location of your phone.
- Unlocking instructions.
- Accounts or apps requiring immediate attention.
- Any additional instructions for managing your digital legacy.

How to Protect Your Phone While Alive

In addition to planning for posthumous access, it's vital to secure your phone against unauthorized access while you're alive. Here are the best practices:

1. Use Strong Authentication

- Enable biometric authentication, such as fingerprint or facial recognition.
- Use a complex password or PIN instead of simple patterns.

2. Encrypt Your Data

Most modern phones offer encryption features to protect stored data. Ensure encryption is enabled in your device settings.

3. Keep Software Updated

Regularly update your phone's operating system and apps to protect against vulnerabilities.

4. Avoid Public Wi-Fi

Use a virtual private network (VPN) when connecting to public Wi-Fi to safeguard your data from hackers.

5. Install Security Software

Use reputable security apps to detect malware and unauthorized access attempts.

6. Be Cautious with Permissions

Review app permissions regularly and revoke access to sensitive information when it's unnecessary.

The Emotional and Practical Importance

For many people, granting access to a cell phone may feel intrusive or unnecessary. However, it's an act of love and foresight. By preparing for unforeseen circumstances, you reduce the emotional and logistical burden on your loved ones during challenging times. It ensures that critical tasks can be completed, and sentimental memories are preserved.

Worksheet: Cell Phone Access and Protection Plan

1. Trusted Person Information

Trusted Person's Name Relationship Contact Information Notes

2. Access Details

Device ______________________________ Location __________________

Unlock Method _______________________________

User ID ________________________ Password ______________________

Notes ____

____

3. Key Accounts and Services

Device ______________________________ Location __________________

Unlock Method __________________________

User ID ____________________ Password __________________

Notes ____

____

4. Posthumous Instructions

- Specific actions for accessing and managing data:

  ____

  ____

Conclusion

Cell phones store critical and sensitive information that can have lasting implications for both personal and financial matters. By securing your phone and planning for access in the event of untimely death or incapacitation, you ensure that your digital legacy is preserved, and your loved ones can manage your affairs with ease.

Taking proactive steps, such as selecting a trusted individual, using digital legacy tools, and documenting access details can mitigate the risks of lost data and unnecessary complications. It's not just a matter of practicality; it's a gesture of care for those who matter most to you.

SPIRITUAL DIMENSION

Objective: Deepen your sense of purpose and connection.

1. **Identifying Purpose:**
    - What are your core values?
    - How do these values align with your daily actions?
2. **Religious Affiliation:**
    - Name of Organization: ______________________________
    - Contact Information: ______________________________
    - Key Beliefs: ______________________________
    - Your Involvement: ______________________________
    - Weekly Support Activities: ______________________________
3. **Mindfulness and Meditation:**
    - Practice a 5-minute meditation focusing on your breath.
    - Write down how you feel before and after the meditation.
4. **Service to Others:**
    - Plan one act of kindness this week.
    - Reflect on how it made you feel and the impact on others.

Religious Scams and Their Impact on Individuals and Families

Religion has been a cornerstone of human societies for centuries, offering spiritual guidance, community, and hope. However, it has also been exploited by unscrupulous individuals and groups to commit fraud. Religious scams manipulate people's faith, trust, and generosity for financial or personal gain. The impact of these scams can be devastating, affecting individuals and families emotionally, financially, and spiritually.

This essay explores the types of religious scams, their profound effects, and the best strategies to avoid them.

Types of Religious Scams

Religious scams take many forms, often tailored to exploit the unique vulnerabilities of individuals who are deeply committed to their faith. Below are the main categories of religious scams:

1. Charitable Donation Scams

These scams prey on people's desire to help those in need. Fraudsters pose as representatives of religious organizations or charities and solicit donations for fabricated causes, such as disaster relief or helping the poor. These scams are particularly effective after natural disasters or during holiday seasons when charitable giving is at its peak.

- **Example:** A scammer impersonates a missionary organization and claims to need funds for constructing a church in a developing country, only to pocket the money.

2. Miracle Cure or Faith Healing Scams

In these scams, individuals claim to have divine or supernatural powers to cure illnesses or solve life problems. They often charge exorbitant fees for their services or require followers to make "seed donations" to activate the healing process.

- **Example:** A televangelist promises miracles for viewers who donate a specific amount to their ministry.

3. Ponzi and Pyramid Schemes in Religious Communities

Some scammers infiltrate religious communities to promote investment opportunities that promise high returns. These schemes rely on new investments to pay earlier investors and eventually collapse, leaving participants financially devastated.

- **Example:** A church member introduces a "faith-based investment" that turns out to be a Ponzi scheme.

4. Fake Religious Products and Relics

Scammers sell counterfeit religious items, such as blessed artifacts, holy water, or prayer cloths, claiming these objects hold miraculous powers. These items are often sold at inflated prices.

- **Example:** A fraudster markets a piece of wood as a fragment of Noah's Ark to unsuspecting buyers.

5. Cult-like Manipulation for Financial Gain

Some religious leaders manipulate their followers into giving away significant portions of their income or assets. These scams often involve psychological control, making victims believe their donations are essential for their spiritual salvation.

- **Example:** A cult leader convinces members to donate their homes and life savings to the organization.

6. Online Religious Scams

The internet has opened new avenues for scammers to target victims. These scams include fake religious crowdfunding campaigns, phishing emails from supposed religious organizations, and fraudulent online ministries.

- **Example:** A scammer creates a fake website mimicking a well-known religious charity to solicit donations.

Impact of Religious Scams on Individuals and Families

The consequences of religious scams are multifaceted, affecting victims on emotional, financial, and spiritual levels. Families often bear the brunt of these impacts, as trust and resources are eroded.

1. Emotional Impact

- **Betrayal of Trust:** Victims often feel deeply betrayed, as the scam exploits their faith and trust in religious institutions or leaders.
- **Shame and Guilt:** Many victims blame themselves for falling prey to scams, leading to feelings of shame and guilt.
- **Emotional Distress:** The loss of money or faith can cause anxiety, depression, and even a crisis of identity, particularly if the scam involved a trusted community or leader.

2. Financial Impact

- **Depleted Savings:** Many victims lose their life savings, leaving them financially unstable.
- **Debt Accumulation:** Some individuals borrow money to contribute to scams, only to face insurmountable debt when the scam is exposed.
- **Economic Ripple Effect:** Families of victims often struggle to recover, leading to reduced quality of life, inability to pay for education, or loss of homes.

3. Spiritual Impact

- **Loss of Faith:** Scams can cause victims to question their faith, leading to a spiritual void and detachment from their religious community.

- **Damaged Religious Institutions:** Scandals involving religious scams tarnish the reputation of legitimate organizations, eroding trust in faith-based initiatives.
- **Isolation:** Victims may withdraw from their communities due to embarrassment or fear of further exploitation.

Best Ways to Avoid Religious Scams

Preventing religious scams requires a combination of vigilance, education, and critical thinking. Below are actionable steps individuals and families can take to protect themselves:

1. Verifying Charitable Organizations

- **Research the Charity:** Use websites like Charity Navigator or GuideStar to verify the legitimacy of a religious organization before donating.
- **Avoid High-Pressure Tactics:** Legitimate charities will not pressure you to donate immediately.
- **Request Documentation:** Ask for detailed information about how donations will be used and verify the organization's tax-exempt status.

2. Recognizing False Claims

- **Miracle Promises:** Be skeptical of claims that require financial contributions for blessings, miracles, or cures.

- **Unrealistic Returns:** Avoid investment schemes promising guaranteed or unusually high returns.
- **Emotional Manipulation:** Watch for language designed to instill fear or guilt to coerce giving.

3. Protecting Personal Information

- **Avoid Sharing Sensitive Data:** Be cautious about sharing personal or financial information with anyone claiming to represent a religious organization.
- **Verify Communication:** Double-check the authenticity of emails, phone calls, or messages claiming to be from a religious institution.

4. Engaging in Open Communication

- **Discuss Decisions:** Talk openly with family members before making significant donations or financial commitments.
- **Seek Advice:** Consult with trusted advisors, such as financial planners or community leaders, when approached with investment opportunities.

5. Strengthening Community Awareness

- **Educate Others:** Share information about common scams within your religious community to increase awareness.
- **Report Suspicious Activity:** Notify local authorities or consumer protection agencies about potential scams.

- **Encourage Transparency:** Advocate for financial transparency and accountability within religious organizations.

6. Seeking Professional Help

- **Legal Assistance:** If you suspect fraud, consult an attorney to understand your rights and options.
- **Financial Counseling:** Work with a financial advisor to rebuild your finances if you've been scammed.
- **Support Groups:** Join groups for scam victims to share experiences and receive emotional support.
-

Worksheets for Identifying and Avoiding Religious Scams:

- **List of Previous Scams Encountered:**
- Company/Individual ______________________________
- Location _______________
- Type of Scam? ___________________________
- Method of scam __________________
- Action taken _____________________________________

  ____
- ____
- **List of Current Religious Organizations You Feel Suspicious Of:**

  Organization _______________________________________

Reason or payment ______________________________

Suspicion ______________________________________

Research _______________________________________

Action Taken ___________________________________

- **Reflection Questions:**
  - What steps can you take to verify the legitimacy of these organizations? ______________________________
  - How has your awareness of scams changed your approach to faith and trust? _____________________

    ____

Confession Brings Possession

Positive Statements for Maternal Wealth

Scripture: "Honor your father and your mother, so that you may live long in the land the Lord your God is giving you." – Exodus 20:12 (NIV)

1. I am surrounded by loving relationships that nurture my emotional well-being and growth.
2. My family bond is built on trust, understanding, and mutual support.
3. I pass down values that inspire future generations to lead purposeful lives.
4. I celebrate the joy and strength that maternal care brings to my life.
5. Every act of kindness within my family strengthens our connection and legacy.
6. I am grateful for the love and care that enriched my emotional wealth.
7. My family thrives on open communication, shared traditions, and unconditional love.
8. I invest time in building nurturing relationships with my loved ones.
9. I honor the lessons and values passed down by my parents and guardians.
10. I am a source of encouragement, love, and care for those around me.

Positive Statements for Spiritual Wealth

Scripture: ***"But seek first his kingdom and his righteousness, and all these things will be given to you as well."*** **– Matthew 6:33**

1. My life is guided by purpose and grounded in unwavering faith.
2. I find peace and strength through my connection to a higher power.
3. My values align with my actions, creating a life of integrity and fulfillment.

4. Gratitude fills my heart as I recognize the blessings in every day.
5. I nurture my soul through prayer, meditation, and acts of kindness.
6. My spiritual journey brings clarity and strength to face life's challenges.
7. I am connected to something greater than myself, providing me with peace and purpose.
8. My faith inspires me to live a life of compassion and generosity.
9. I embrace mindfulness and find joy in the present moment.
10. I trust that God's plan for me is good and brings abundant blessings.

Positive Statements for Financial Wealth

Scripture: ***"The plans of the diligent lead to profit as surely as haste leads to poverty."*** **– Proverbs 21:5**

1. I make wise financial decisions that align with my long-term goals.
2. My financial resources empower me to live a life of stability and purpose.
3. I manage my money with discipline, gratitude, and responsibility.
4. I use my financial wealth to support my family and contribute to my community.
5. My income and investments grow steadily, creating security for my future.
6. I am proactive in creating opportunities for financial growth and success.
7. I balance spending, saving, and giving to reflect my values and priorities.
8. I trust my financial plan to lead me toward abundance and freedom.
9. I am grateful for the financial blessings I have and share them generously.
10. My financial wealth supports a legacy of empowerment, love, and purpose.

These affirmations provide focus and positivity for each dimension of wealth, fostering growth and gratitude in maternal, spiritual, and financial aspects of life.

Conclusion

Religious scams are a betrayal of trust that exploit people's faith and goodwill. They can have far-reaching consequences, damaging individuals, families, and even entire communities. By understanding the types of scams and their impact, individuals can take proactive steps to protect themselves and their loved ones. Education, vigilance, and open communication are the keys to avoiding these fraudulent schemes and maintaining faith in both spiritual and financial matters.

Religious communities and leaders also have a role to play in fostering transparency, accountability, and awareness to safeguard their members from exploitation. Together, these efforts can minimize the prevalence of religious scams and their devastating effects.

Personal Journal

By Dennis Doboyouh

Personal Journal

Personal Journal

Personal Journal

Personal Journal

By Dennis Doboyouh

Personal Journal